Sea Island Blues

Library of Congress Catalog Data

Daye, Tyree
Sea Island Blues. Poems
ISBN 978-0-9915514-2-2 (paperback)

Book design by Crystal Simone Smith

For author inquiries or for information about permission to reproduce
selections from this book contact:

Backbone Press, Inc.
PO Box 51483 Durham, NC 27717-1483
backbonepoetry@gmail.com

www.backbonepress.org

Table of Contents

When I was New

When I was new to loneliness
and the burn liquor,
I walked Carolina streets
looking for a pretty face
to take home and tell me
with a half-moon smile
she never loved you.

The small cedars and pines dancing
under street lamps celebrated
a night without lightning.
And I danced with nothing but gin
in my stomach, Robert Johnson
in my head,
the devil in my wallet.

When you're poor hell is the least
of your worries. It's a hard thing to kick,
loneliness, without drugs or booze.
The angels of sleep press your silhouette
on the wall across the room.

And I heard a Geechee woman sing a song
that flew up like cardinals we were told
to blow kisses at for good luck.
We sat on a live oak branch
that hung men and women
who cried freedom in G major.

Tenki, tenki Gawd fuh keepin' me.

Life is harder than bottom-barrel gin.
And when bone sprouts from under skin

we water it in hallelujahs. A man in a pressed suit
goes amen. Some miles down the road another sinner is born.

Around the Praying Tree

Sitting among the live oaks watching
Spanish Moss blow in the southwest wind.

Its silent songs can only be heard by the marsh,
and tonight I wanted to see a ghost so badly,

a soldier from the 54th charging our steps,
his locked eyes singing glory hallelujah,

the scars on his back fresh and stinging.
A whole congregation holding hands in prayer

around a loblolly pine, the weight of their songs
pressing against the thin branches.

Croker

for my mother

Before she chops the arrow-shaped head off,
before the meat pushes through
white as Sea Island Cotton, she scrapes the scales from one side
breaks and then scrapes it again and thanks Gawd
for the fish and waterways. The men still
drunk from last night's homemade wine sit back
on quiet porches where they can see the moon in
the day time, when they need something that feels like
a blessing, to thank something or somebody.

Before my mother would yell
dinner time, dinner time
she would throw salt on rice again
for good measure. Dinner time, dinner time, come and eat.
The sun hid half her face as we sat around
the hand-me-down table, the brown wood grew wings, and
turned golden in sunlight. Our table was always quiet, hunger
made knots out of our tongues and what prayer do you
send to Gawd when you hardly believe anymore and sleep
feels like the only thing you own.

Return

When you walk into a still-standing slave cabin
you hold back tears. For the first time it becomes real.
The second is when you try to sleep that night
and behind your eyelids you are arranging bodies
to imagine how twelve people could fit
in so small a space. And then you think you can see their faces
and are confused as to why they're laughing.
You don't understand until a year later
when the land calls you back.
Their means of survival did not idle and die.

In 1850 I would have sold for 825 dollars.
In today's market, quiet like the songs of
blackbirds, that's around 36,000.
That's if my hands moved fast enough
along the rows of fine cotton and the scars on my back
touched the front of my soul's stomach.
The older ones have the gray hairs full of memory
shaved from their faces. We are all fed well on auction day.
The day you may never see your mother's brown eyes again
is the same day you're given a new pair of pants and told
to stand up straight.

1847

I put Spanish Moss in my shoe
and learn the notes to *Wade in the Water*,
not to lower my blood pressure, which it does,
but to go back to 1847. I've prayed the most I ever have
this week and held back tears.
Bloom where you're planted. Gawd walks the light to you.
How many songs rose and fell under this old oak.
So many notes collected in its bark
I believe I can hear them now.

Where Barefoot Farms meets Indian Hill
you still can hear the word *liberty*. Just as much
as you hear *hallelujah*. Here the dead walk upright
beside the living and on Fripp Island
they dig sinkholes under
million-dollar homes while the night reflects
off the ocean and turns itself blue.

Bury me by the water and
when the tide raises, pray it carries me
home. Why do we think we can one up
Gawd? The angels sit on oak branches
and laugh at our golf courses and weep
for the land. Grab my shotgun and *holla*
when you hear them coming. My mama
was buried here and her mama too.
They sang Swing Low and watched
Horseshoe crabs, living fossils, die, so the next group
could live on. We are no different, don't turn your back

to the marsh. Out here the land moves with the water and has no sympathy for anyone.

1862: At the Penn Center Looking at the Children's Photos

"If we die let it not be like hogs" Claude McKay

I looked into their faces.
Where do the young boys eyes go
when the museum closes? I can't forget them.
Him eye long, they follow me to sleep
then to dreams that wake me
wanting water. Their father's hands
couldn't get a break. The earth
swallowed everything they planted
and birthed a singing weed. *E done learn
a heap of ting* about the feel of dirt,
the sharp cotton bolls that cut to the snowflake colored bones.
If a quilt was made to show my life from birth to death
let a dark sky full of stars sit in the middle,
to remind them that's all I ever wanted.

My Country Song

I went home to wild dogs and Sun Tea where
the little dipper sits right above a row of eighty year-old pines,
where following the North Star doesn't lead to freedom
anymore but you can follow it and still get killed. It's nice to
talk to someone who says it's not just you. Both of us learning
ain't no glory in the bottom of those bottles, just more country
songs. Tonight my Uncle, the one they say look most like my
granddaddy, staggered on beer and said the Lord's Prayer and
before we said our amen my knees buckled in and I want to
say it was the devil coming out of me, but it wasn't.

Praying

My mother washed our white clothes in Clorox,
the bleach would eat holes in our shirts and
show the bright brown underneath.
Most everybody I know is stuck
in a gin bottle and Gawd's too late
to get them out. We saw you walk into
a healthy pine once and laughed, those
would be tears now. They would sweep you down the street
and you would struggle in the current and forget you were a
man. You would smile like children do in death.
Still so close to that side.

Right now the late afternoon looks like it did
when Sal took those belts to the stomach
and howled all night, until Gawd let him sleep.
Cardinals call out over
the low hum of the highway,
cooling from a hell-going hot week
that rested on bent brown backs in the soybean fields.
Until the boss man tells the backs to straighten up
and go home only a few Lumbars pop into place, but
all of them are thinking of how they need to get back
to something they truly remember
and haven't blocked out
or left outside to bark at distant lights,
the bats dancing in mid-air, wings shaped
like bass clefs, the world singing an old gospel hymn
that starts and stops throughout the night.
Maybe one of our favorite aunts will cook
our favorite pies and someone
will say amen and we all will feel it.

Jimmy's Prayer

Queen Quet said the Klan never rode on St. Helena,
never saw the Four Corners or Indian Hill.
Out here the crosses are fire proof.
Shotguns remain loaded and polished, a Gullah man
knows where his land ends and another begins
by whatever tree has grown there. Gawd speaks and sings
through everything. *Call em out 'E name,*
is shouted in praise houses. When the clouds
cover the stars just enough
for some light to push through. *Call em out 'E name.*
Those voices must stretch as far as the Sierra Leone
and all of King's Highway purses, when black gold
shows just how golden it is.

When you rest your hand on the Chapel of Ease
and feel its sharpness, its points,
you can almost match your breathing
with the building's. As if every hand that made the tabby,
mixture of lime, sand and oyster shells,
came back to finally enter its walls to praise.
During the Stono Rebellion a head was placed on a
pole at every mile marker and traveling back home
I imagine every one. Every face said keep running,
the North star is the brightest
for a reason.

Rambling on my Mind

When the light reaches every eye.
When survival is written in A Major.
A meeting on the front porch just to look across the land.
Grandmamma lived to look at you and match faces.
Every year the elders leave us with a song.
When they sing Amazing Grace you leave your shoes
and stand on the smile of oldest man there, 101 years.
We never made eye contact. He knows
the rising of the tide by feeling.
We get our own prayer out in the wood and return with a
shield.
When you seek in dim summer twilight the stars pulse
and we inhale them before oxygen.

Nothing ever came of my drunk late nights,
maybe a lie or two about how her eyes met my own
and how she mouthed something that looked kind.
Not even the neighbors cared about my cry-cry blues
that played nonstop. Every woman's and man's gut *holla* out
over a twelve bar scale. Her softness can only be felt.
E' hears the blessing of a people.
The shadow I'm in doesn't feel true.

After the night showers leave to drown
some other half-made town,
nothing touched has grip. Tractors remain
stuck in stubborn mud.
A coma might be better than death.
Sometimes that feels like all I need, a long sleep.

Riding the Bus into Raleigh

There's no dirt road with two children on opposite sides
like crows, who run because it feels good.

No bubbling city block that when quietness comes
it scares off pigeons and makes everyone look up.

There's no country church lost in hallelujahs, no city temple
that can fully see or not see the Nat Turners.

I hope my vision from Gawd comes in the form of familiar
hands and not the gin bottles we hold like new life.

You see faces but never remember them.
Struggle is a thick cloth tied around our wide-open eyes.

Why do E' Visit Cemeteries?

E' visits to talk and laugh with grandmas and uncles.
To catch a breeze from the water.
To leave mama's favorite cooking spoon.
To bring pictures of the newest baby of the family,
resting in her daddy's arms.

The Story of Mud

Mud covers everything,
you can't smoke a Camel without covering
the green tip of the filter with it.
Rolling a tire out of the marsh, hurrying
before the tide comes. I found an army of crab
among the thick roots of an oak. They disappeared as fast
as I spotted them, anarchy spreading among the ranks.
They must've of heard about me from a group of seagulls
and when they told the story their wings opened
and lifted them off the ground a little.
How when I was twelve I shot a blue jay
from a tree and didn't check if E' was alive.

Aluminum is the saddest material
when it doesn't shine anymore, the
sun breaks from its corners and lies there.

Neuroplasticity

Winning a basketball game almost
makes you forget you're poor. We are not the children of
bible readers. Performing a sin for rent money is a daily thing.
Watching my mother gather what she could keep of warmth
before entering the cold is easy when you're young.
The pink sky over her is an urn, we are trapped.
We mirror dope boys with cell phones.
Dialing a number that could be their last.

I hope there's a familiar song at the end
and not the hell I dream about. You can only
tell a man he's gonna see heaven after this thinly sliced
life so many times before he decides hell
would make a better story.

Any Black Southern Poor Boy's Blues

I'm no choir boy, no
preacher's son. Fasting is never done
on purpose. Gin or thighs helps me sleep
and both make me forget me for a moment.
Most nights she tells me she loves me,
others blanket us in silence, when even our orgasms
don't speak. I like Saturday night fixes,
whatever Johnny brings back from New York City.

I'm no choir boy, no preacher's son.
I learned how to shoot a rifle when I was twelve
and found out what being black could get you.
When you kill a hog you put the bullet behind his ear
and split him open from the top of belly down.
Sixty pounds of meat can feed at least 100 people.
You get the grill real hot before you lay E' up there.

I know the feel of church pews
and the smell of *reefer*. I know how to
balance a checkbook and cash bad checks.
I drink my coffee black and like my
women any color like my uncle told me
it's all pink on the inside

A Meeting at the Praise House

The oldest leads the song.
Gawd's favorite chord is an
E. The note that best speaks
fuh da soul.

Come now children feel
the sun on your back,
call out. Let all the world
know your light.

The Seeking

The secrets are held and hidden
in hands that shaped the landscape.
Walking the streets alone,
I listen for Jimmy's African drum
and thank Gawd I found no trouble
waiting in a Dixie red pick-up. I watch three
police officers roll the state flag
in the traditional way. The birds sing in the same key
as the Star Spangled Banner. Every breeze here
come from the southwest. First cooling
the old slave massa houses sitting on
the bay. Those porches cry million-dollar tears.

America doesn't want this story.
This story has no smiling darkies
ready please. This is a number one man's story, who'd fetch
at least 1,400 on the auction block. This is
an ordinary girl's story, this is Omar Ibn Said's story.
These stories traveled by railroad,
river, world of mouth, coffle. Through the
finger tips of a sweet grass weaver
humming hymns into the threads of the basket.

We got different opinions about trees
and freedom is spelled Gawd.
Tonight wanting to drink these stories away
I'll go to the wood in my head
and began my seeking.

Gentrification

We don't need a scientific method. We
don't need to know how far the stars are but we
know them like kin. We
measure a baby's weight
by placing them in the palm of our hands. We
love we.

We the poor folks at the bottom of the hill
can hear the rich coming like a river.

When Birds Sing Love Songs

Once a blackbird flew into our house
and my grandmother died the next week.
I try to tell myself the two days didn't
connect tissue to bone, it didn't form a body.

We came home and found the family in circles
congregated in the front yard, some sitting, some standing.
Crows above them as witnesses to the death. They reported
to the Ash trees and they sees their swaying for a moment.

I want this to be a love poem, about socks
and how we lose them in nights
of twisted sheets and legs.
And how we find them weeks later
unharmed and still touching.

My mother tells me I was a sweet child,
sugar crusted. Until my Uncle who often played
my father on dull hardwood floors, chased a woman
into a dream and never came out.

Never gathered his baseball caps
from the shelf, to take with him.

Prison Poem #2: Or Our Stories in the Key of E

I never understood your love for the color red.
Until she walked to the door turned around
and asked would I be ok. Even the moon behind her
is leaving. My mother keeps reminding me that
poverty and booze don't mix and can kill any man.
I wanted to send you poems to cover all the gray
surrounding you, but I never did.

What do we do with all these stories of
pond fish and dog fighting, getting caught
smoking behind the shed and me hiding by the pond,
everyone thinking I fell in?
Learning that crack smells like burning oil
from our uncles Chevy, that the summer heat
and a woman that doesn't love you can bust a
mans heart?

List of Terms

E: Gullah/Geechee can mean person (male or female) or thing.

Gawd: God

Coffle: a group of people or animals chained, tied together and driven along

Tabby: concrete mixture made from lime, sand and oyster shells

About the Author

Tyree Daye was raised in Youngsville, North Carolina a small town with two main roads leading in and out. He is a student majoring in creative writing at North Carolina State University. He will graduate in December of 2014 and plans on continuing studies in a MFA program. He is influenced by poets Etheridge Knight, Larry Levis, and Lucille Clifton. He believes that poetry has allowed him to be honest with himself and the world. It allows one to turn chaos into beauty.

Acknowledgments

Grateful to the following journals where the poems have appeared:

Connotations Press: *"My Country Song"*
Prairie Schooner: *"Jimmy's Prayer"*, *"The Story of Mud"*, *"This Black Southern Poor Boy's Blues*
San Pedro River Review: *"Neuroplasticity"*, *"When Birds Sing Love Songs"*, *"Prison Poem #2: Or Our Stories in the Key of E"*
"Croker", winner of the 2014 N.C. State Undergraduate Poetry Prize.

Gentrification: written in honor of Gwendolyn Brooks,
We Real Cool.

Thank you to my mother Joyce Anne Glover, Dr. Dorianne Laux, Joseph Millar, Dr. Tracy Ray, and Robert E. Green.